W9-BRH-686

21st-Century
Engineering Solutions
for Climate Change

RISING TEMPERATURES

KAITLYN DULING

Cavendish
Square

New York

Published in 2019 by Cavendish Square Publishing, LLC
243 5th Avenue, Suite 136, New York, NY 10016

Library of Congress Cataloging-in-Publication Data

Names: Duling, Kaitlyn, author.
Title: Rising temperatures / Kaitlyn Duling.
Description: First edition. | New York : Cavendish Square, 2019. |
Series: 21st-century engineering solutions for climate change |
Includes bibliographical references and index. | Audience: Grade 7-12.
Identifiers: LCCN 2017056418 (print) | LCCN 2017060331 (ebook) |
ISBN 9781502638342 (ebook) | ISBN 9781502638328 (library bound) | ISBN 9781502638335 (pbk.)
Subjects: LCSH: Global warming--Juvenile literature. | Global temperature changes--Juvenile literature.
Classification: LCC QC981.8.G56 (ebook) | LCC QC981.8.G56
D85 2019 (print) | DDC 363.738/746--dc23
LC record available at https://lccn.loc.gov/2017056418

Editorial Director: David McNamara
Editor: Kristen Susienka
Copy Editor: Rebecca Rohan
Associate Art Director: Amy Greenan
Designer: Alan Sliwinski/Megan Mette
Production Coordinator: Karol Szymczuk
Photo Research: J8 Media

The photographs in this book are used by permission and through the courtesy of: Cover and page 1 Lukas Schulze/Getty Images; p. 4
UIG/Getty Images; p. 8 US EPA/File: Earth's greenhouse effect (US EPA, 2012).png/Wikimedia Commons; p. 10 © 2008 Public Library
of Science/File: Ice age fauna of northern Spain/Mauricio Antón.jpg/Wikimedia Commons; p. 13 Slowking4, own work/File: People's
Climate March 2017 in Chicago 4290240.jpg/Wikimedia Commons; p. 16 Someone35, own work/File: Melting glacier (Skaftafellsjökull).
jpg/Wikimedia Commons; p. 21 Fotoluminate LLC/Shutterstock.com; p. 26 Rob Atkins/Photographer's Choice/Getty Images; p. 28 M
Day Photography/Shutterstock.com; p. 29 Haywiremedia/Shutterstock.com; p. 32 Prisma Bildagentur/UIG/Getty Images; p. 36 US Forest
Service/https://inciweb.nwcg.gov/incident/photographs/5564/File: 2017 09 06-23.51.59.187-CDT.jpg/Wikimedia Commons; p. 40 Abd.
Halim Hadi/Shutterstock.com; p. 43 Andy Barrett, own work (User: Big Smooth)/File: Mt Hood Natl Forest.jpg/Wikimedia Commons;
p. 48 Robert Kirk/Moment Mobile/Getty Images; p. 51 Photorush, own work/File: Sequoyah Nuclear Power Plant.jpg/Wikimedia
Commons; p. 60 Nairobiphoet, own work/File: The Boys and The Cows.jpg/Wikimedia Commons; p. 62 Anthony Kwan/Getty Images.

Printed in the United States of America

CONTENTS

CHAPTER ONE

IT'S GETTING WARMER

Whether you're watching the nightly news, listening to the weather on the radio, or scrolling through the headlines online, it's hard to miss the phrases "global warming" and "climate change." While Earth's temperature has never been steady or stagnant, the last couple of decades have brought increased public awareness of global warming, the effects it is currently having on the planet, and the ways in which it can affect Earth's climate in both the near

Opposite: A layer of smog and fog blankets the Hollywood Hills in Los Angeles, California.

and far futures. We can't escape talking about how our atmosphere is heating up—and we shouldn't.

Understanding Differences

It is essential, from the start, to understand the difference between "global warming" and "climate change." Global warming describes the heating up of the planet—an increase in Earth's temperature over time—mainly due to increasing greenhouse gases in the atmosphere. This is one aspect of climate change. Climate change describes a change in Earth's overall climate over time. This can include changes in precipitation patterns, natural weather disasters, and extreme drought. You can think of it like this: global warming is the cause and climate change is the effect.

Another key point to remember throughout discussions of these two topics is that today when scientists, public leaders, and members of the media speak and write about global warming and climate change, they are often referring to human-caused warming. This is warming caused by the rapid increase in greenhouse gases due to human activity.

A greenhouse gas, of which carbon dioxide, water vapor, methane, and others are examples, is a gas that absorbs heat and radiates it back to Earth, creating global warming. See how that works? These gases don't just appear out of thin air. Humans create them every single day through manufacturing and transportation, among other activities. The burning of coal, oil, and gas leads to the creation of greenhouse gases. These gases escape into Earth's atmosphere, where they absorb the heat radiating from Earth and keep that heat trapped within the atmosphere.

/ DID YOU KNOW? /

We didn't always use the phrase "global warming." In fact, "climate change" didn't come into academic or popular use until the late 1970s, with the publishing of a decisive study that used the phrase. For the next several years, the words were used interchangeably. But in 1988, a NASA scientist testified before Congress about the climate, specifically using the phrase "global warming." Since then, the use of "global warming" in media and popular discourse has grown.

It's Getting Warmer

Because the heat enters the atmosphere and then stays inside, we call this process the greenhouse effect. A greenhouse keeps heat inside even when the temperature outside is cold. This allows plants to grow all year long. But on Earth, we don't need to trap heat inside! When this happens within our atmosphere, it can cause major climate changes across our entire planet.

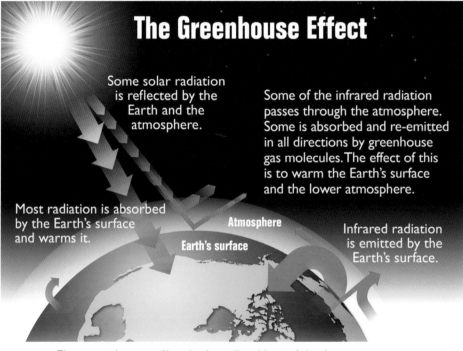

The greenhouse effect is described here. It is always happening, even if we can't see it from Earth.

Is It All Our Fault?

While global warming is most often understood to be caused by humans, many people are split over the causes of climate change. Historically, climate changes have occurred due to both human causes and natural evolutions in Earth's climate. Earth's average temperature has fluctuated over time. With a history of over four billion years, you can bet there have been some minor and major changes!

Humans can change the climate through methods other than the greenhouse effect. Aerosol pollutants are tiny particles that cool the climate as they reflect sunlight. They are released into the atmosphere through burning coal, oil, and forests. Whenever we change Earth's landscape in a major way—by planting forests or cutting down trees to make more farmland, among other things—the climate can be affected.

Earth has also experienced hot and cold periods throughout its history, and some people believe that we are transitioning into another change in climate. The cold periods are usually called ice ages, while times of warming are called interglacials. These run on a roughly one-hundred-thousand-year cycle. If you look at a global temperature map that spans hundreds of thousands— or even millions—of years of Earth's history, you will see a jagged line that goes up and down many, many times. Earth's temperature has never stayed constant.

The big question is, what is causing the climate changes we are beginning to witness today? Is the increase in heat-trapping gases that humans add to the atmosphere truly causing global warming, and is this something we can slow down or possibly reverse? Or are we in a time of natural warming, an interglacial? Do we need to change our behavior, or can we keep up with our rapid, constant rate of industrialization across the globe? These questions

Many ice ages have occurred in our planet's long history. This illustration imagines what it was like in the last ice age.

THE INDUSTRIAL REVOLUTION

The greenhouse effect is directly impacted by pollution from manufacturers. Everything from automobile factories to steel production sites to power plants produces pollution that escapes into Earth's atmosphere. Today's booming industries didn't appear out of thin air. The transition into a more technologically advanced, factory-oriented society is known as the Industrial Revolution. This period, which began in Great Britain, extended from roughly 1760 to the 1830s. As manufacturing became more efficient and developed, new sources of air and water pollution emerged. These effects weren't limited to Great Britain, however. The Industrial Revolution occurred in North America as well, and the resulting innovations soon spread across the globe, ensuring that pollutants would continue to enter the atmosphere at a quick pace over the course of the next two centuries.

are at the forefront of today's debates surrounding global warming and climate change. Until we can come to places of understanding and agreement in these conversations, nothing can be done to combat global warming. Without solutions, all we can do is wait and see.

Believers, Skeptics, and Deniers

If you talk to your family, friends, peers, and others, you will likely hear many different thoughts and opinions about the nature of global warming and climate change. It is difficult to deny that climate change is happening. We can see it in the natural disasters, such as hurricanes, floods, and tsunamis, that continue to strike, and strike hard, around the globe. We can measure the melting ice caps in the Arctic as well as the rising sea levels. We can detect changes in ecosystems, greater numbers of certain pests, and long periods of drought. These are real, physical manifestations of the rising temperature of Earth. However, people cite a diverse array of causes when discussing the driving forces behind climate change. The majority of scientists argue that human

Demonstrations like this one in Chicago in 2017 help get the word out about the dangers of climate change.

activity is the main cause of global warming and that we should be alarmed. Some are skeptical, suggesting that there are natural causes for the warming. Certain groups are neutral on the causes but believe that we are able to adapt, and that we should not be alarmed. Still others deny altogether the existence of global warming and even climate change.

While one could argue that climate science is cut-and-dry, certain factors make the whole story much more complicated: Earth's long history, and all the weather, warming, cooling, disasters, and more that have happened over billions of years. Today, scientists have pinpointed the accelerated temperature changes over the last century and attribute those to human activity. However, some deniers reject mainstream scientific opinion and instead argue that no climate change is happening whatsoever. Instead, they suggest an "urban heat island effect." This effect is real—urban areas can measure warmer temperatures due to human activity—but deniers specifically argue that these urban measurements account for global warming and thus should have no bearing on the choices we make as a global people when it comes to our climate. Other skeptics point toward historical weather patterns. They note that temperatures are changing but claim that any temperature change is entirely natural and should not be a concern of the public. The solar cycle, volcanic activity, Earth's orbit, deforestation, and natural ozone pollution are just a few of the "natural" sources of global warming and/or climate change put forward by skeptics.

Global warming and climate change have become hot-button political issues. At the extreme end, some groups deny that climate change is happening at all, or don't want to discuss the "why" and believe deeply that, no matter what happens, we can adapt as our climate changes.

But scientists remain certain that the greenhouse effect is being driven by human activity. It is caused by driving cars, burning fossil fuels, creating electricity, producing goods, and so much more. Scientists think if we work hard, we can both mitigate and adapt to climate change. Mitigation refers to stabilizing the levels of greenhouse gases already present in the atmosphere by reducing the emissions we put out. Adaptation addresses the impacts of climate change that are already present on Earth by adjusting the ways in which we live. According to most contemporary scientists, both responses are needed in order to address this global problem.

/ DID YOU KNOW? /

Climate models are systems that use data and mathematical equations in order to simulate things that could happen in our world and atmosphere. These are often called GCMs, short for global climate models.

CHAPTER TWO

CLIMATE CHANGE TODAY

If we know one thing for sure, it's that our planet is heating up. Through measurements and observable changes, we can see clearly that Earth is undergoing a period of warming. Most scientists agree that the main cause is human activity, resulting in the greenhouse effect. Others tend to disagree, arguing that there are natural patterns behind the warming. Remember, gases involved in the greenhouse effect

Opposite: This glacier in Iceland is melting. As our planet warms, glaciers like this will continue to melt.

include methane, carbon dioxide, nitrous oxide, and others. They each result from different activities, both natural and caused by humans. From these gases, we can gather a more complete picture of the causes of global warming. Then, we can take a look at how that warming is affecting our planet through climate change.

Causes

When you listen to people on television, the internet, or in day-to-day life talk about global warming, they are apt to point out a number of different causes. Some say Earth's temperature is rising naturally due to the sun or historic cycles that we should already expect. Others point to human causes—manufacturing, transportation, and other processes that involve the burning of fossil fuels. In truth, global warming is due to a combination of different factors. To get a clear picture of what causes global warming, we first need to understand, at a basic level, the gases present during the greenhouse effect.

Carbon dioxide (also called CO_2) is released in many ways. It leaves us when we breathe out, through a process called respiration. It is released when volcanoes erupt. Human activities that release carbon dioxide into the atmosphere include deforestation, land use change, and the burning of fossil fuels. We burn fossil fuels when we drive cars, produce electricity through the burning of coal or natural gas, manufacture cement, and so much more. Since the Industrial Revolution, people have been burning fossil fuels at ever-increasing rates, sending more and more carbon dioxide into the atmosphere.

Methane is a hydrocarbon gas produced when fossil fuels are extracted from the earth as well as when they are burned. However, methane is distinct from CO_2 in that it is also released during agricultural activities. Intensive livestock farming, such as "factory farms" found in the United States, have driven an increase in methane levels in the atmosphere. Animals like cows, sheep, and goats are called ruminants. They create large amounts of methane due to the fermentation that occurs during their normal digestion processes. In this way, meat eaten every day has a huge impact on methane emissions and global warming. Similarly, landfills and waste create millions of tons of methane each year. When microbes in garbage break down waste, they naturally create and emit methane. The decomposition process continues for years, even after a landfill is closed. Other sources of methane include wetlands, termites, biofuels, rice production, and biomass burning.

Nitrous oxide is a very powerful greenhouse gas. One of the main sources of nitrous oxide emissions is the use of synthetic fertilizer for agriculture. Microbial processes in the soil treated with synthetic fertilizers produce the nitrous oxide. It is then released into the atmosphere. Animal waste management systems are affected by the same microbial processes as the soil, making livestock manure another source of nitrous oxide. Additionally, biomass burning, fossil fuel combustion, industrial processes, and human sewage all release nitrous oxide into the atmosphere.

Fluorinated gases are synthetic compounds used inside refrigerators, air conditioners, aerosol cans, and more. These gases are often contained within equipment and products, and their leakage causes emissions during their usage, as well as during their manufacture and maintenance. As entirely human-created compounds, these gases have the potential to be completely discontinued from use. You may have heard of them in relation to the ozone layer, as they contribute to the destruction of this atmospheric layer. Internationally, steps have been taken to reduce their common use (such as the use of aerosol cans) due to the destruction of the ozone, but they are still present in various products and industries.

Water vapor is known as a "feedback" greenhouse gas. This means it amplifies the warming effect of all the other greenhouse gases. It is also a greenhouse

Livestock like cows are a major source of methane gas.

gas itself, absorbing energy as it radiates from Earth. As the atmosphere gets warmer, it can hold even more water vapor. This additional water vapor absorbs even more energy, and so on. This is sometimes referred to as a "positive feedback loop." Unlike the other greenhouse gases, more water vapor isn't produced through specific human activities but through global warming itself. As the atmosphere heats up, its humidity does as well. So the more we allow the greenhouse effect to occur, the more water vapor will enter the atmosphere, in turn amplifying the greenhouse effect.

As you can see, the greenhouse effect is caused by a multitude of activities—both natural, like volcanic eruptions, and human, like the burning of fossil fuels to produce electricity. In addition to these causes, there are a few other drivers of climate change that have been identified by scientists and researchers, such as solar irradiance and ocean-atmosphere variability.

Solar Irradiance

The sun is the major source of energy that drives Earth's climate. Both those who believe deeply in humans' effects on the climate and those who are skeptical have expressed that the sun plays a role in climate change—at least on a historic level. By studying historic models, researchers have been able to pinpoint that increases and decreases in solar activity have triggered ice ages and other significant changes over time. However, those who deny that humans are exacerbating the greenhouse effect have pointed toward solar activity time and time again, ignoring several pieces of evidence that make clear the sun's minimal effect on today's temperature changes.

Ocean-Atmosphere Variability

In addition to solar activity, oceans can also affect the climate. Some who deny that humans play a part in climate change point toward El Niño-Southern Oscillation (ENSO) as one of the true causes. ENSO is a periodic variation in sea surface temperatures and winds that occurs over the eastern Pacific Ocean. Its effects are usually felt in the tropics and subtropics. El Niño refers to warming periods, while La Niña denotes the cooling phase. The periods last a few months and occur irregularly.

Outside of El Niño and La Niña, the oceans naturally redistribute heat between their depths and the atmosphere all the time. This can lead to changes in surface temperature. Discussions of ocean-atmosphere variability inevitably lead to a chicken-or-the-egg situation. Is El Niño causing climate disasters and weather events, or is the warming planet changing the behavior of El Niño? Climate scientists, politicians, and the general public have yet to reach consensus on this.

Effects

No matter the cause of global warming, the consequences of a warming planet are impossible to ignore. Climate change across the globe is both observable and measurable. Some of the changes were predicted decades ago, while others have come as a surprise. But all of them are due to the warming global temperature, and that is only expected to rise if we don't take quick and serious action. According to the Intergovernmental Panel on Climate Change (IPCC), a temperature rise of 2.5 to 10 degrees Fahrenheit (1.3 to 5.5 degrees Celsius) over the next century is probable. The IPCC has also stated that "the range of published evidence indicates that the net damage costs of climate change are likely to be significant and to increase over time."

It's true that scientists are extremely concerned about what life on Earth will be like over the next few decades and centuries if the planet continues to warm at current rates. But before we even begin to surmise what will happen in the future, we have to take a look at the current state of affairs: What can we observe and measure in order to see the effect that climate change is already having on our world?

One of the most-circulated statistics when it comes to warming is, of course, the temperature! Earth's average surface temperature has risen about 2°F (1.1°C) since the late 1800s, around the time that the Industrial Revolution occurred in Europe and North America.

Many argue that today, the global temperature change has continued to increase due to human activity, especially industrial activity. Evidence shows most of that warming occurred over the last thirty-five years, in the late twentieth and early twenty-first centuries. This evidence is entirely measurable and fairly indisputable. Even when we experience snowstorms, chilly rainfall, or colder-than-average seasons, the planet is, overall, undergoing a period of warming.

What We See in the Weather

Due to the rise in global temperature, much of the planet has seen a steady increase in extreme weather events. Heat waves, times of abnormally hot weather that can last for weeks, and droughts, times of abnormal dryness, are two of the most common ways that people are affected by global warming. In 2011, portions of Texas and Oklahoma experienced over one hundred days that were over 100°F (37°C). Due to the heat, water sources were depleted, and agriculture was negatively affected. The states had billions of dollars in direct financial losses due to loss of agricultural revenue.

In what might seem like the opposite effect, many regions have also experienced an increase in heavy rainfall. In the United States, the Northeast and Midwest have been hit with increasingly heavy

Heat maps like this one help us "see" the rising temperatures and predict how warm it could get in the future.

downpours and major flooding over the last few years. Heavy rainfall is directly related to increased water vapor in the atmosphere, which we know is connected to the greenhouse effect. Storm systems have access to this water vapor, resulting in rain that falls heavy and fast, causing flood conditions. Floods can also be caused by hurricane, snowmelt, or the failure of dams and levees. Floods damage property, ruin crops, and threaten the lives of people living in flood-affected areas.

Weather events like major floods can devastate entire neighborhoods and cities. This neighborhood in Texas flooded after Hurricane Harvey in 2017.

Since the early 1980s, there has been a major increase in hurricane activity in the Atlantic Ocean. Hurricanes produce strong winds and form over warm ocean waters, though they have been known to make landfall, especially in recent years. Over the last few decades, hurricanes have become more frequent, more intense, and longer. The number of Category 4 and 5 storms (the two most severe levels) has increased. It is simple to link increased hurricane activity to global warming, as hurricanes form and move through areas with higher sea surface temperatures. These can vary naturally but are also affected by global warming and other forms of pollution, such as particulate pollution. Scientists are still working to determine the amount of influence the natural and human-caused factors have on hurricane formulation.

Like hurricanes, heavy rainfall, heat waves, and droughts, winter storms have also increased their frequency and intensity over the course of the last century. This might seem counterintuitive, but it all fits together. In 2006, during a warm winter blamed on global warming, Lake Erie did not freeze for the

Winter storms can trap families inside their homes.

first time in its history. That year, more evaporating water from the lake was available for precipitation, leading to increased snowfalls throughout the region. When the atmosphere holds more moisture in general, leading to heavier precipitation, that naturally includes heavier snowfall under winter conditions. In the Northern Hemisphere, snowfall has been shifting northwards. Fewer snowstorms have been occurring in the southern United States, while heavier-than-normal snowfalls have been happening in the northern Midwest and far Northeast over the last few years. This is due, in part, to the warming Arctic. Warmer air in the Arctic actually drives winter storms south, pushing them into North America and Europe.

Other Evidence

As anything heats up, it is natural to expect some melting. Globally, we are seeing a rapid decrease in the size of the polar ice sheets—they are melting, fast. The ice caps are mainly found in Antarctica and the land around the Arctic Ocean, including Greenland. Polar satellite measures of these ice caps began in 2002. Between that year and 2011, results showed that nearly all of the polar regions were losing ice. Over twenty years, Greenland alone lost 152 billion tons (138 billion metric tons) of ice. Even though it gains ice back in the winter, it is shedding ice so fast in the summertime that the losses cannot be made up. Its ice sheet is shrinking. However, it's not just ice sheets. Glaciers are melting too, affecting the habitats of Arctic animals (like seals and polar bears) and adding even more to the mass melting that is occurring at either pole of the planet.

All of that melting ice has to go somewhere, and it's flowing into Earth's oceans. Since 1992, polar ice loss has contributed nearly 0.5 inches (12 millimeters) to the global sea level. Although it might not seem like much, more rapidly melting ice will add to this and could lead to devastating consequences. As the seas move higher, homes, businesses, families, and animals will be displaced.

In the United States, sea levels are rising quickly on the East Coast and near the Gulf of Mexico. Since 1880, the global average sea level has increased by 8 inches (20.3 centimeters). Higher seas can also give a boost to heavy storms and even add to the greenhouse effect by replacing white, reflective ice with dark ocean water. Dark water absorbs more heat than white ice. As the ice melts, all of the dark water that is produced absorbs more and more energy from the sun. This causes a warming effect. The warming oceans and continued melting of land ice will create higher and higher rises in sea level, affecting even more humans, animals, and the places we call home.

While the sea levels continue to rise, putting vulnerable communities at risk, the oceans are also experiencing advanced acidification, or changing chemistry of the water, due to global warming.

Delicate coral reefs have become threatened by rising temperatures. This reef has suffered coral bleaching.

COMBATING MISINFORMATION

While the solutions for mitigating and adapting to climate change abound, one of the most low-tech solutions that organizations today are focused on is simply combating misinformation. Organizations like the National Park Service (NPS), the Union of Concerned Scientists, and others have dedicated themselves to educating the public about the realities of global warming and the changing climate. Research universities, government agencies, and other groups are working hard to produce data, while the NPS and educational organizations are focusing on educating youth and families. It takes daily work to set the record straight in the popular press, advocate for climate legislation, fight back against attacks on scientists and research, and expose special interest groups who misrepresent scientific information.

When we put CO_2 into the atmosphere, some of it is absorbed by the world's oceans. There have been some historical benefits to this, but scientists have recently discovered that there's a downside: acidification, specifically the reduction of seawater pH (a measure of acidity). A lower pH denotes a more acidic environment, which can have a dramatic effect on coral, sea urchins, clams, oysters, and other sea creatures. If and when these animals' lives are disrupted by acidification, it won't just impact them alone. It will change entire ecosystems and could potentially put entire coral reefs at risk of disappearing.

The oceans aren't the only large areas affected by climate change. Forests are also feeling the pains of a warming planet. As everything heats up, we are beginning to see more forests ablaze, especially in the American West. This is due to a variety of factors. On one hand, global warming can lead to higher temperatures and drier conditions: the perfect combination for a forest fire. Other human activities, such as land use, mining, and development, can further increase the risk for forest fires. The fires are becoming even more difficult to contain. Large, intense fires will probably be felt more frequently if Earth continues to warm at its current rate or faster.

With all of those ecosystems falling apart—glaciers melting, coral reefs disappearing, wildfires destroying forests—the next occurrence we can expect, and that we can witness right now across the world, is the movement of animals from one place to another. Some animals, like migratory birds, move between different places every year or every few years. According to the Audubon Society, safe habitats for birds are already shifting and changing. This is due to development in their natural habitats, an increase in natural disasters, and changes in precipitation and temperature, and we can expect

DID YOU KNOW?

In October 2017, California experienced catastrophic fires. Over 40 people were killed, 90,000 were forced to evacuate from their homes, and an estimated 8,900 structures were destroyed. Heavy winds and high, dry temperatures contributed to the fires, which also destroyed much of northern California wine country.

Roaring wildfires, like this one in northern California, can destroy homes and pose a danger to people.

migratory patterns to shift right along with them. Think about the geese you see flying south when the weather turns cold and north in the springtime. A recent study noted that spring is arriving as many as twenty days early across much of the United States. Will changes in seasonal temperatures change the times of year when geese fly and where they travel to? Potentially. In turn, changing migration patterns will affect the food that the birds eat, and those animals that prey on different species of birds.

Additionally, we can see other types of animals moving to other areas as the climate changes, redistributing themselves in order to find new ways to thrive. For instance, mosquitoes are now able to live at higher elevations, bringing malaria with them onto mountain slopes where it used to be nonexistent. In South Africa, diamondback moths have expanded their range, eating up the cabbages, kale, and cauliflower planted by poor urban farmers who never had to worry about the pests before. Moose and hares have moved farther into the Alaskan Arctic, even crossing the 600-mile (1,000 km) Brooks Range in northern Alaska to feed on shrubs that now grow feet higher than they used to due to warming temperatures. But the people who live and hunt in northern Alaska don't mind—as melting sea ice makes seals harder

DID YOU KNOW?

Rising temperatures aren't just putting animals on the move. They're also changing breeding seasons. Scientists have found that frogs and other amphibians around the world are breeding about eight days earlier, on average, with each decade that passes. Over time, this adds up, changing the natural rhythms of an entire habitat.

to chase, they have begun to subsist on the moose and hares. In a National Geographic Society tally of more than four thousand species around the globe, about half of them are shifting their range right along with climate change.

It is important to remember that while much of this evidence is observable and measurable right now, scientists are even more concerned about how these effects will continue to grow and change in the future, as the planet warms even further. If we continue to allow the atmosphere to heat up our planet by even a few degrees, we will be feeling these impacts in a huge way. We will experience even more disastrous weather events, and on a daily basis we will bear witness to changing ecosystems and climate through the food we eat, the industries we support, the cities where we live, and so much more. If we are at all discomforted by the changes that are already here, we must take action now to slow or reverse global warming, while also adapting to the mess it has already made. If we don't, we may be in for more problems than we ever expected, needed, or wanted.

MODELING THE PAST

Climate models can give us a window into the past. Today, archaeologists and researchers at Washington State University are utilizing computer modeling to learn how ancient cultures dealt with changes in the climate. They are tracking the choices made by ancient cultures in Asia, North America, and elsewhere that led the societies to fail or thrive. Using models, they can see what worked and what didn't between virtual families and specific simulated environmental changes, such as precipitation and reduced resources. "Crop niche modeling," focusing on agriculture, allows researchers to identify which crops grew during times of drought in particular areas. This type of crop modeling can help contemporary society find drought-resistant crops, such as Hopi corn, that may be crucial to human survival in the future.

CHAPTER THREE

MODERN ANSWERS AND INNOVATIONS

With just the quickest look around, we can see that our planet is warming. We can feel it, touch it, bear witness to its steady rise in temperature. Through data measures we can pinpoint the causes—including but not limited to the greenhouse effect. We can make elaborate computer models that peer into the future, giving us a glimpse into what life might be like on Earth in the coming decades if we don't make substantial changes. So many of our daily choices and societal structures need to change in order to adapt

Opposite: People cope with rising temperatures in many ways. This man in Malaysia is drinking a large bottle of water to stay cool.

to climate change in the coming years. Even bigger changes need to be made if we wish to mitigate, or reduce, the occurrence of global warming and climate change.

Mitigation

Mitigation refers specifically to efforts to reduce and stabilize the levels of greenhouse gases in the atmosphere. Currently, carbon dioxide is removed from the atmosphere by natural processes in places like forests, oceans, and savannas. These places are known as carbon sinks. They naturally accumulate and store CO_2 at varying levels. However, the rate of removal by natural processes is only about half the rate of current emissions from human activity. If we seek to stabilize emissions at their current rate, we will limit the rate of global warming, but we will not reduce atmospheric concentrations of greenhouse gases. We need to take further actions in order to truly reduce levels and make a noticeable difference in the world. These actions need to be both aggressive and sustained, and they need to happen on a global scale.

Forests, like the one sprawling before Mount Hood in Oregon, can act as powerful carbon sinks.

One of the clearest and most substantial ways we can mitigate global warming is by reducing the burning of fossil fuels for electricity, heat, and transport. The burning of fossil fuels releases greenhouse gases into the atmosphere, causing global warming and, in turn, producing harmful climate changes. If we can reduce or altogether stop the burning of fossil fuels, we can significantly reduce the climbing levels of CO_2 and other gases in the atmosphere.

We have many options when it comes to reducing fossil fuel use. One of the most significant sources of fossil fuels is manufacturing. Since the Industrial

Revolution, factories have been huge sources of greenhouse gases. Pollutants are emitted during the manufacturing process and during the extraction of materials, like oil, that go directly into consumer products. But factories also use electricity every day. Believe it or not, electricity contributes the most greenhouse gases in the atmosphere. That's because electricity is most often generated by the burning of coal or natural gas at power plants. Both coal and natural gas emit greenhouse gases. Factories and people use electricity every day. Every time you turn on the television, charge your phone, turn the lights on, or step into a warm shower, you're using electricity, which has most likely been produced through the burning of fossil fuels. In our daily lives, we each contribute directly to global warming. So, can we change that? Of course!

Changes in fossil fuel consumption can start with a change of behavior: turn off the lights when you leave a room; reuse your old items instead of buying new ones; purchase CFL (compact fluorescent) or LED (light-emitting diode) light bulbs to replace your old, energy-using incandescent bulbs. A quick online search will give you hundreds of ways to reduce your energy consumption at home.

In some US states, consumers have the option to choose the source of the electricity that powers their home. With the click of a button, homeowners and renters can choose traditional coal and natural gas, 100 percent renewable energy, or a mix of both. Some suppliers even allow consumers to choose the type of renewable energy they want. In this way, families and business owners can make a real, sustained impact on global warming.

Today, renewable options are becoming cheaper and more accessible by the day. The two main sources of renewable energy in the United States are solar power and wind power. Sometimes these

DID YOU KNOW?

When measured by ton of oil equivalent (toe), or the amount of energy released by burning one ton of crude oil, some countries consume much more energy than others. China consumes the most energy: 3,123 million toe (Mtoe) in 2016! The United States is second, with 2,204 Mtoe.

are called "alternative" energy sources because they are technically an alternative from coal and natural gas. However, unlike coal and gas, wind and solar do not produce harmful greenhouse gases during the electricity-generation process, and they do not necessitate mining for a substance that is in limited supply. Wind never runs out! And the sun's energy is here to stay, at least for the foreseeable future.

Solar and Earth-Born Power

The twenty-first century has seen a rise in many different energy solutions, but one of the most well known might be solar energy. Today, you might see a small solar panel powering a stoplight or a field full of panels that powers a factory. At its most basic, solar panels turn energy from the sun into energy that can

/ DID YOU KNOW? /

According to researchers at the American Society of Heating, Refrigerating and Air Conditioning Engineers, 70 percent of electricity in the United States is used for buildings. This makes up more than 40 percent of total energy used in the country.

Solar panels are a clean and efficient option for power at home.

be used to power all kinds of things in one's home or business. This can be done in a couple different ways. Photovoltaic cell technology converts sunlight directly into an electric current. In a solar thermal process, solar energy is used to make steam. Then, the steam is converted into electricity through the turning of a turbine. Solar energy is entirely clean and renewable—it doesn't produce greenhouse gases, and it doesn't run out. Even on cloudy days, we can rely on the energy stored within solar panels. One downside to solar power is probably its expense. The panels remain relatively expensive to produce, purchase, and install, and they haven't become as popular as many would have hoped. However, the price falls a little bit each year. As global warming continues to heat up the planet, we may see solar panels become a more popular energy solution.

Just like we can derive energy from the sun, we can also generate electricity from water. Hydropower and geothermal energy harness moving bodies of water and the energy inside Earth to produce electricity. Likewise, biomass can be used as a form of relatively clean, renewable energy. Biomass refers to the use of agricultural waste and other wastes to generate electricity.

Wind

In today's market, wind stands out as a simple, beautiful, and nearly limitless form of energy generation. You may have seen wind turbines dotting a flat field or perched on a coastline. These machines convert the kinetic energy inside wind into mechanical power. The wind turns the blades of the turbine, powering an electric turbine that then supplies an electric current. This is the opposite of a fan. The turbine uses natural wind to make electricity—without putting greenhouse gases into the atmosphere. It is entirely clean and renewable, and it can also be transported. Many wind turbines in downstate Illinois power the densely populated city of Chicago, hundreds of miles away. As the costs go down each year, more and more states in the United States, as well as other countries across the world, are investing in wind as a form of sustainable energy.

Altogether, wind, solar, hydropower, geothermal, and biomass make up the top five most commonly used renewable energy sources in the United States. Unfortunately, none of them have the market share or popularity that coal and natural gas continue to hold. The coal industry, especially, has tons of money, lobbyists, special interest groups, politicians, and history behind it, ensuring that coal mining remains a big part of American life, as well as life around the globe. Even though the burning of coal accounts for a huge share of CO_2 emissions and creates harmful air pollution, many people believe that the loss of coal would only create negative outcomes for their communities, especially when it comes to the loss of jobs. When discussing energy solutions, one cannot ignore the power of history and culture. Many small towns in America were built on coal mining and remain proud of their relationships with coal. It will take more than a little prodding to transition from this CO_2-emitting process to alternative energy sources that can produce the jobs, energy, and sustainability that we so badly need.

Nuclear

When it comes to mitigating greenhouse gases, renewable energies like wind and solar are great solutions to move toward, but they've only gained popularity in the last few decades. Before those took off, people were already talking about another form of alternative energy—nuclear power. The first nuclear power plant was built in Russia in 1954. Since then, nuclear power has gained in popularity. It has been promoted as a safe, efficient, and clean alterative to coal and natural gas. Unfortunately, almost since their conception, nuclear power plants have been the site and cause of many major disasters that not only harmed people living in the affected areas but

Nuclear power plants emit steam—not smoke—from their cooling towers.

released radioactive gases into the atmosphere, ensuring that their harmful effects would be felt years into the future. Due to these disasters, nuclear energy hasn't become as popular as some may have thought it would. And it isn't as "clean" as many promote, either. The mining, extraction, transportation, and refining of uranium all use electricity, for which we still need to burn fossil fuels. Fossil fuels are used to build nuclear reactors, process the waste the reactors produce, and transport that waste. In the next few decades, it will be up to us to decide what exactly "clean" means, and what level of emissions is "too much."

Carbon Sinks

It is not only imperative that we investigate alternatives to our current forms of energy production, but we must also search out ways in which we might reduce the levels of CO_2 in the atmosphere. One of the ways we are currently doing this, and could continue to do in the future, is through the protection and support of natural carbon sinks. These are the areas such as forests, oceans, and savannas that accumulate and store greenhouse gases that would otherwise be released into the atmosphere and contribute to the greenhouse effect. A carbon sink always absorbs more carbon than it releases. The reduction of CO_2 in the atmosphere due to carbon sinks is sometimes called negative emissions.

One of the best examples of a carbon sink is a forest. Canada, the United States, South America, and some Asian countries such as Indonesia have very large forest interests. In these countries, it has been suggested that the planting of new forests (a process called reforestation) take place in an effort to combat global warming. Unfortunately, there are a couple factors that make forests less than ideal as carbon sinks. First, when they burn, forests release even more stored carbon into the atmosphere. As Earth warms, we are likely to experience more forest fires, which means more carbon releasing. The planting of forests has been criticized as a "quick fix" solution that doesn't promote emissions reduction or lead to an actual reduction in emissions, because even after the forest is built, consumers and companies won't necessarily be motivated to change their behaviors. We can already see this dynamic play out when large companies—some of them fossil fuel companies—help fund forest planting that doesn't even begin to offset the emissions released by their main money-earning activities.

Soil is another option for carbon sinking. Over the last 150 years, we've seen many of the world's grasslands tilled into farmable fields and pastureland. These fields naturally sequester, or store, carbon. In fact, the conditions that make carbon sequestration most efficient and powerful in soil match up perfectly with the conditions for organic farming. However, most farmable land is currently used for large-scale, industrial-style farming that utilizes harmful chemicals and pesticides rather than chemical-free, natural organic methods. It may take decades before we see real changes in farming that can lead to large-scale carbon sequestration in soil.

Carbon Capture and Sequestration

One of the newer technologies being suggested to combat global warming is through a type of artificial carbon sink—carbon capture and storage (or sequestration), also known as CCS. In this process, the carbon dioxide is captured from smokestacks when coal is burned. Then the CO_2 is injected into the earth instead of being allowed to release into the atmosphere. While this is an extremely new technology, the US federal government is currently subsidizing the coal industry's efforts to develop and expand it. Currently, there is only one coal plant in the United States using CCS. It is still expensive and under research, making it unlikely to become a popular practice anytime soon. CCS also has many vocal critics, some of whom are concerned about the effects of CCS on natural underground water sources, plate tectonics, and more. Though the CO_2 will be buried instead of released as a greenhouse gas, it will still be present within our planet, and scientists aren't 100 percent sure what will happen to it once it's underground. Some scientists have suggested injecting the CO_2 into the ground at the bottom of our deepest oceans. However, the high pressure of the deep ocean, the presence of bacteria, and the presence of marine life present many possible implications. To many skeptics, CCS sounds like a risky move to take, whether it's in the ground or beneath the ocean!

Climate Engineering

Another innovative solution that has been put forward in the climate change discussion is still in the theoretical stages. Climate engineering (or geoengineering) refers to a group of largely hypothetical techniques for manipulating the global climate in order to stabilize or reduce the effects of climate change. These efforts are advanced and actually differ in a subtle but key way from both mitigation and adaptation. While adaptation seeks to help us endure climate changes and mitigation focuses on reducing greenhouse gas emissions, climate engineering works to moderate and/or forestall the effects of climate change. The study of climate engineering has increased drastically in the last decade or so, due in no small part to the continual, rapid rise in our measures of global temperature. The federal governments of the United Kingdom, United States, and Germany have all commissioned assessment reports on the topic. Geoengineering solutions generally fall into two camps: the idea to remove greenhouse gases such as CO_2 from the atmosphere, and the attempt to reflect sunlight away from Earth, causing Earth to absorb less solar radiation. Either of these solutions would be large-scale, deliberate, and far-reaching. Scientists usually suggest climate engineering as an accompanying strategy to both mitigation and adaptation, though the ideas themselves remain highly speculative and are nowhere near the implementation stage.

Adaptation

Now that we've explored possible solutions for mitigating global warming, we must also look to another proposed way of dealing with the changing climate—adaptation. This refers to adjusting to the current and future climate, both on a personal and a societal/global level. Extreme effects of climate change, many of which we can already see, such as rising sea levels, destructive weather events, and food insecurity, make us vulnerable to harm. It is the goal of adaptation to reduce this vulnerability. Adaptation also seeks to take advantage of any possible "pros" or benefits of climate change. Longer growing seasons and increased crop yields are two examples.

Today, substantial adaptation planning is occurring at all levels of global government, as well as in the private sector. These plans come with barriers: limited funding, political roadblocks, and the difficulty of anticipating climate changes, even with all of our technology-rich models. We can't always tell when a disaster might strike, how hard it will be felt within communities, or if our levees and dams can hold up to increased and increasingly unpredictable levels of precipitation. In these cases, adaptation is often reactive, happening after climate changes have already affected us. However, it is possible for us to adapt proactively in order to prepare for the ways in which we know (or at least predict) our climate will change.

Adaptation Through Government and Policy

Governments at the local, state, and federal level, as well as international coalitions, have all taken steps to proactively and reactively adapt to changes in Earth's climate. Government arms such as the EPA and the NPS in the United States have stepped up their education, research, and advocacy efforts in order to prepare citizens for climate changes. Of course, as government leadership changes hands along with the election cycles, it is yet to be seen if those efforts will remain in place.

When it comes to mitigating and adapting to climate change, some countries are leading the way. In 2015, Sweden committed to eliminating the use of fossil fuels within their borders. Today, only about 20 percent of Sweden's energy consumption comes from the burning of fossil fuels. Costa Rica has also been working to eliminate reliance on fossil fuels. In the first few months of 2017, the country produced 99 percent of its energy through renewable energy sources. Germany and Nicaragua are also pushing ahead with strong commitments to renewable energy. Even China, the world's largest emitter of carbon, has become a leader in solar panel and wind turbine installation, working to keep up with its enormous population and even greater energy use.

In tropical areas around the world, local governments, nonprofit organizations, and international coalitions have teamed up to take a stand against deforestation. For tens of thousands of years, indigenous groups have populated tropical forests. Today, their homes are being threatened by governments and corporations that seek to destroy natural forests in favor of logging, cattle ranching, soy farms, and other activities. Deforestation on a large scale threatens not only human communities but also wildlife and ecosystems. If we can curb the cutting down of these tropical forests, we can cost-effectively and quickly help to curb global warming. These forests can act as large, powerful carbon sinks as well as homes for people, animals, and plants.

Climate models tell us that if tropical forests were reduced to fields, a drier, hotter climate would result. Some even predict that the continued destruction of tropical forests will alter rainfall patterns as far away as China and northern Mexico. Organizations like Greenpeace, the Sierra Club, and the International Conservation Union are partnering with policymakers in Southeast Asia, the Pacific Islands, West Africa,

Developing communities are trying to adapt and respond to climate change.

FUNDING SOLUTIONS WHERE FUNDS ARE SCARCE

Unfortunately, it isn't easy to secure funding to mitigate and adapt to climate change in the developing world. Some organizations, noticing this problem, have stepped in to help. Groups such as the World Resources Institute and the Adaptation Fund are working to provide direct access to funds for developing countries through research, recommendations, advocacy, test projects, and partnerships. These funds will help organizations within those countries complete projects such as investing in climate-smart agriculture (water control to minimize risks from floods and droughts) in the West African country of Guinea-Bissau and building adaptive capacity in vulnerable indigenous communities on the border of Columbia and Ecuador.

South America, and other regions in order to slow or stop the deforestation of these important forests.

Additionally, a president has power when it comes to a country's involvement in international agreements. In 1992, the United Nations adopted the Framework Convention on Climate Change (UNFCCC). This treaty set nonbinding limits on greenhouse gas emissions. It didn't set up any mechanisms for enforcement, so it wasn't the most hard-hitting or useful legislation, but it did serve an important symbolic purpose. The countries that signed on to the UNFCCC were making a statement about their dedication to working to

French president Emmanuel Macron (*left*) and German chancellor Angela Merkel (*right*) meet at the UN Climate Change Conference in 2017.

combat climate change. Since the UNFCCC, other treaties tied to the original document have sought to set binding terms on nations. The 1997 Kyoto Protocol set targets for some (but not all) signing countries. Most recently, the 2016 Paris Climate Agreement aimed to limit the global temperature increase. Many countries have signed the accord. However, a lead contributor, the United States, had yet to fully commit as of 2017.

Many local governments have taken an interest in climate change adaptation. In fact, most adaptation efforts have occurred at the local and regional levels. A 2011 survey of 298 local US governments showed nearly 60 percent engaged in some form of adaptation planning. Some governments have put in provisions to protect infrastructure (such as protecting roads and sewers from flooding) and maintain existing ecosystems. Others have begun regulating the design and construction of buildings in their communities and encouraged more emergency response preparedness. Construction regulation includes building higher homes and roads in flood-prone areas. In some of these areas, it's not unusual to see houses built up on tall stilts! Today, some governments are even purchasing homes from those who live in flood zones rather than risking even more disasters. Land-use planning is another way that local governments are working to adapt. When they think about how land can be used, be it by new forestland, organic farms, industry, or residences, they have an opportunity to consider carbon sinks and carbon producers. When they approve new skyscrapers, they can push for green roofs that include plants, specific energy-absorbing materials, and other "green building" characteristics.

Innovative Solutions

In addition to mitigating and adapting, there are new and exciting technologies that seek to tackle climate change on both an individual and a global level.

One proud investor in climate change–tackling technology is Ben & Jerry's Ice Cream. In 2014, Ben & Jerry's reported that they had invested in a manure separator for their cow farm. The machine separates manure solids and composts them into sanitary bedding for the livestock, reducing 50 percent of their methane output. A company called NativeEnergy provided the funding for the project in exchange for carbon offsets. Essentially, this means that NativeEnergy regularly produces an amount of greenhouse gas pollution and was able to pay for the chance to "offset" their pollution, investing in carbon reduction projects in the developing world. Carbon offsets like these could ultimately lead to fewer greenhouse gases entering the atmosphere, but detractors just call this system an ineffective distraction. Opinions remain split. For now, the cows at Ben & Jerry's are sleeping on recycled bedding that will keep about 11,000 tons (10,000 metric tons) of CO_2 out of the atmosphere over the next decade, all thanks to businesses making solutions that were good for business.

Can cars create energy even as they burn fossil fuels? Some scientists think so! One of the most recent power-generation concepts is road power generation. This turns the energy of moving vehicles into electric energy through the installation of special plates on the road. When a car's wheels strike the road, they create a rotary motion that generates electricity that can be used to power businesses, stoplights, streetlamps, and more. This type of technology has also been used in speed bumps placed near drive-through windows, tollbooths, and at the entrance to large events like circuses. These speed strips have been tested throughout the United States but have not yet come into popular use. Across the globe, a similar system has found a home in bicycle-heavy Amsterdam, where SolaRoad, a bike path version of the electricity-making road idea, has already generated enough energy to power a home for an entire year.

Traditional cars rumbling over speed strips might be able to produce electricity, but some roads themselves are able to charge electric cars! You may have seen special parking pads at gas stations that charge electric cars without plugging them in. Now, researchers are working on roads—real life "electric avenues"—that will use complex coil systems to charge electric vehicles as they drive. Some of this technology is already being used in South Korea, where electric buses use small batteries to cover their routes and are able to recharge at bus stops along the way.

Today's large passenger airplanes use gasoline and release huge amounts of greenhouse gases directly into the atmosphere whenever they fly. However, aircraft designers and scientists are coming together to create alternative flying options. For example, researchers at NASA are working on alternative designs for commercial aircraft that use low-carbon propulsion technology. Engineers are also trying to design airplanes that fly with electric power.

What does it take to "go green," or be environmentally friendly? For architects and builders, there is a clear set of standards for "green," or sustainable, building practices. The US Green Building Council introduced Leadership in Energy and Environmental Design (LEED) a few years ago, and it has taken off. LEED is the primary green building rating system in the world. It not only rates buildings after they are built, but most importantly, it provides a framework for building teams during the design process, helping to create healthy, efficient, cost-saving structures that produce little to no greenhouse emissions.

Cool roof technology reaches past the local government level, all the way down to the level of the consumer. Made of highly reflective materials, so-called cool roofs are designed to reflect sunlight and absorb less heat. This is similar to the way light-colored clothing can make you feel cooler on a hot day. Cool roofs decrease the need for air conditioning, reducing energy use; reduce the urban heat island effect if enough buildings in an area have them; lower peak electricity demand in a city, which can help to reduce power outages; and can even absorb CO_2 if they are covered with plants.

Research has overwhelmingly demonstrated that we need both adaptation and mitigation in order to deal with climate changes now and in the future. The two efforts are very closely linked. Without mitigation, adaptation will remain costly, difficult, and much less likely to succeed. If we can combine mitigation, adaptation, and even new innovations like geoengineering or other solutions, we may be able to find hope of a cooler future for our warm planet.

CAN AN APP COMBAT CLIMATE CHANGE?

Some innovative solutions to global warming and climate change can be found right in your pocket! Companies that make applications for smartphones have been churning out some helpful new products over the past few years. Many of these can help consumers cut down on their carbon footprint and save fossil fuels. Some, like ridesharing apps Uber and Lyft, encourage carpooling and less car ownership. More people in one car means fewer fossil fuels are being burned than if all the people in the car drove their own car. There are also carbon emissions trackers to see just how much carbon your next car or plane trip will release. The app Farmstand helps you find local farm stands and co-ops where you can buy produce grown close to home. NASA's Earth Now app even allows you to see real-time models of our warming planet.

acidification The changing chemistry of water.

carbon capture and storage The process of capturing carbon dioxide from fossil fuel power plants and depositing it underground.

carbon offsets A reduction of carbon emissions in one place in order to compensate for emissions made elsewhere.

carbon sink A material or location that captures and stores more CO_2 than it releases into the atmosphere.

climate engineering A group of largely hypothetical techniques for manipulating the global climate in order to stabilize or reduce the effects of climate change.

fluctuate To rise and fall with irregularity.

fluorinated gases Synthetic gases, including those that contribute to the greenhouse effect.

fossil fuel A natural, nonrenewable fuel derived from the remains of ancient living organisms.

greenhouse gas A gas that absorbs radiation and radiates heat, contributing to the greenhouse effect.

Industrial Revolution A period of major economic and social changes that took place between the late 1700s and the early 1800s and was marked by revolutions in manufacturing, agriculture, and transportation.

kinetic energy Energy produced from motion.

methane A gas produced during agricultural activities, as well as when fossil fuels are extracted from the earth and burned.

negative emissions The reduction of CO_2 in the atmosphere due to carbon sinks.

nitrous oxide A colorless gas, often used as an aerosol propellant, that contributes to the greenhouse effect.

particulate A very tiny, separate particle, often composed of dust or soot.

pH A measure of acidity.

reforestation The planting of new forests, often to act as carbon sinks.

ruminant A mammal, including cattle, sheep, deer, and giraffes, that chews the cud regurgitated from its compartmentalized stomach.

synthetic compound A man-made substance, rather than one produced naturally.

water vapor The gaseous phase of water.

Books

Barnard, Bryn. *The New Ocean: The Fate of Life in a Changing Sea*. New York: Knopf Books for Young Readers, 2017.

Bergen, Lara. *The Polar Bears' Home: A Story About Global Warming*. New York: Simon and Schuster, 2008.

Sneideman, Joshua, and Erin Twamley. *Renewable Energy: Discover the Fuel of the Future with 20 Projects*. White River Junction, VT: Nomad Press, 2016.

Walker, Sally M., and Tim Flannery. *We Are the Weather Makers: The History of Climate Change*. Somerville, MA: Candlewick Press, 2010.

Websites

American Museum of Natural History: Climate Change

https://www.amnh.org/explore/ology/climate
-change

On this site sponsored by a Smithsonian Museum, you can learn about climate change through games, stories, videos, and hands-on activities.

Center for Climate and Energy Solutions: Climate Basics for Kids

https://www.c2es.org/science-impacts/basics/kids

This site covers climate basics, as well as what we can do to help.

National Geographic Kids: What Is Climate Change?

https://www.natgeokids.com/au/discover/geography/
general-geography/what-is-climate-change

This site outlines the causes of climate change and how people can expect to be affected.

SELECTED BIBLIOGRAPHY

Bennett, Jeffrey. *A Global Warming Primer: Answering Your Questions About the Science, the Consequences, and the Solutions.* Boulder, CO: Big Kid Science, 2016.

Benoit, Peter. *Climate Change.* True Books: Ecosystems. New York: Scholastic, 2011.

"Confronting the Realities of Climate Change: The Consequences of Global Warming Are Already Here." Union of Concerned Scientists. http://www.ucsusa.org/global_ warming#.WgAC9RNSxE6.

Hoster, Harry. "Wired-Up Roads Will Soon Charge Your Electric Car—While You're Driving." *The Conversation*, February 8, 2017. https://theconversation.com/wired-up-

roads-will.-soon-charge-your-electric-car-
while-youre-driving-72625.

Kilkenny, Nancy Smith. "Researchers Advance
Propulsion Toward Low-Carbon Aircraft."
NASA.gov, January 4, 2016. https://climate
.nasa.gov/news/2383/researchers-advance
-propulsion-toward-low-carbon-aircraft.

"National Climate Assessment." US Global
Change Research Program. http://nca2014
.globalchange.gov/report#section-1946.

Pidcock, Roz. "Analysis: What Global CO_2
Emissions Mean for Climate Change Goals."
CarbonBrief, November 15, 2016. https://
www.carbonbrief.org/what-global-co2
-emissions-2016-mean-climate-change.

Romm, Joseph. *Climate Change: What
Everyone Needs to Know.* New York:
Oxford University Press, 2016.

Roston, Eric, and Blacki Migliozzi. "What's
Really Warming the World?" Bloomberg

Businessweek, June 24, 2015. https://www
.bloomberg.com/graphics/2015-whats
-warming-the-world.

Shaftel, Holly. "Global Climate Change: Vital
Signs of the Planet." NASA, November 1,
2017. https://climate.nasa.gov.

"What Is Acidification." PMEL Carbon Program.
National Oceanic and Atmospheric
Administration: US Department of
Commerce. https://www.pmel.noaa.gov/co2/
story/What+is+Ocean+Acidification%3F.

Worthington, Daryl. "Solutions to Climate
Change Found in Archaeology." New
Historian, December 22, 2016. http://www
.newhistorian.com/solutions-climate
-change-found-archaeology/7762.

INDEX

Page numbers in **boldface** are illustrations.

ABOUT THE AUTHOR

Kaitlyn Duling believes in the power of words to change hearts, minds, and, ultimately, actions. An avid reader and writer who grew up in Illinois, she now resides in Pittsburgh, Pennsylvania. She loves to learn about and advocate for a healthy, sustainable environment.